The 3-Space Reverb Framework

Framework

Learn the step by step system for using
reverb in your mixes

Nathan Nyquist

The 3-Space Reverb Framework:

Learn the step by step system for using reverb in your mixes

ISBN: 9781980673606

Table of Contents

Introduction

Reverb is the most important tool for creating the perception of space in a mix. Without it, mixes would sound flat and lifeless.

When I first started using reverb, I had no idea what I was doing. There were tons of presets to flip through, and for some reason I felt like I had to tweak everything about them.

If I had gotten over my ego sooner and realized that presets are creative catalysts, along with access to a book like this, then I would have mastered reverb much quicker.

I want for you to feel comfortable tweaking reverb and to feel just as comfortable using presets, because they are one of the fastest ways to discover something new.

If you aren't yet fluid with reverb, I'm going to give you my powerful 3-Space Reverb Framework which will allow you to easily setup reverbs and get straight into the production process.

It's very easy to get sucked down the wormhole of engineering and not actually producing a song. We've all been there. We can spend so much time tweaking this and that parameter, mistakenly thinking that this is what the experts are actually doing.

But the truth is, the experts usually make about 1-3 'main' adjustments within a preset before moving on.

There's a story that reminds me of this fact. It follows the owner of a factory who hired an engineer to fix an expensive machine. The engineer walks in, taps the machine in a couple spots and then grabs a hammer and hits it once and the machine is fixed.

The owner asks the engineer how much for his services to which the engineer says, "$1000." The owner scoffs, saying "but all you did was hit it with a hammer!!!"

A discussion follows and they end up agreeing that he'd pay whatever it was as long as he was given an itemized list.

Later that week he received the itemization list in which was listed as follows:

Hammer: $5

Knowing where to hit the machine with hammer: $995

I bring this up because this book is about knowing where to hit the machine with a hammer. In any plugin or hardware processor there's an infinite number of combinations. It's easy to get sucked into the tweaking trap if you don't know what you're after.

This book is going to make it crystal clear what you're after and how to achieve it so that you can spend the rest of your efforts simply making 1-3 big adjustments and then continuing forward.

Creativity is forward movement, not the circular, swirling, vortexy, black-death movement that is characteristic of getting stuck in unproductive loops.

So the reason I wanted to write this book, is because I think reverb is the one tool you shouldn't be spending too much time tweaking.

But *it is* the most important tool to know **how to use**. That's because it's responsible for creating almost the complete entirety of the perception of depth and space in your mixes.

Put simply, reverb is the environment that your mix takes place in.

It's weird to say that reverb is the environment that your music takes place in because you can only be in one environment at a time, and if a single reverb creates one environment, then why is everyone using multiple reverbs in their mixes? Strange isn't it?

The reason we use multiple reverbs is because in any mix there is only so much room for noises. I refer to this as mixing real-estate. If you use more real-estate than you've got, then you get a Greek tragedy of a mix.

Different reverb types take up different amounts of mix real estate, and so it's important to make sure you use the right reverb types in your mix. We we'll be categorizing reverb types and showing you how to use them throughout this book.

In order to effectively conserve mixing real-estate we are going to be using 3 reverb types in my 3-space reverb mixing framework. They are as follows:

1. **Short-decay reverb**
2. **Medium-decay reverb**
3. **Long-decay reverb**

The reason for these reverb types is because different reverbs take up different amounts of mix real-estate.

As you'll notice, the **decay** descriptor refers to the length of the reverb or how long it takes for its reverberance to fade into silence. We'll go much deeper into this later on.

Using these 3 types of reverb together will create the entirety of your songs environment.

Even though it's probably obvious, I want you to understand that a single reverb will simulate the space of 1 environment. The reason we are using 3 reverbs together is mainly because it affords us better control over our mixing real-estate.

To be even more specific the reason we are using 3 reverbs is because of long-decay reverbs. Here's why.

Long-decay reverbs naturally take up the most mixing-real estate because anything that feeds into them lasts forever.

So the 3 reverbs types take up different amounts of space. This means that the longer the decay of the reverb, the more space it will take in your mix. Our mixing-real estate says there is only so much space in a mix, so we want to use it carefully.

The longer the decay the more real-estate that reverb is going to take.

So in order to efficiently and expertly control our mixing real estate which means how much our reverb fills it up, we need to have a simple strategy for using these 3 styles of reverb together.

Throughout this book I'm going to be showing you how you use these 3 types of reverb I mentioned earlier and how to put them together to create the total environment of your mix.

Once you learn my 3-Space Reverb Framework you'll be able to flip through presets (or make your own) and make adjustments very quickly.

So now let's talk about 3-Space Mix Theory because it's the foundational paradigm from which the 3-Space Reverb Framework operates.

Paradigm #1: 3-Space Mix Theory

3-Space Mix Theory is the foundation of my 3-Space Reverb Framework.

I divide the entire space of a mix into 3 zones or regions called the **Front, Middle and Back Spaces**.

Each space of the mix refers to a positioning of sounds. The way that I envision it is if you were to stand at the front of a movie theater next to the screen and face the seats. As you face the seats you could imagine placing your instruments in different rows of the theater.

Instruments in the Front row would be in the **Front Space**, in the Middle Row would be the **Middle Space**, and in the Back would be the **Back Space**.

You'll notice I often sequence it front, back, and then middle.

That's because the middle is always configured relative to the front and back spaces. I always recommend figuring out your front and back space reverbs first, and then configuring the middle so it fits between them. This is the most natural and intuitive way to efficiently configure reverbs.

Now going back to our imaginary theater, the **front**, **middle** and **back** rows will each have their own unique reverb. It's going to be the specific configuration of each reverb for these 3 spaces in our theatre that will create the entire perceived environment of our mix.

As you'll learn later on, the way in which we configure reverb for each of the 3 spaces in our mix will be done so that they sonically contrast.

The reason we're aiming for distinct sonic differences between each of these 3 reverbs is because it multiplies the magnitude of perceived space within our mix.

When you start using my 3-Space Reverb Framework you'll notice an immediate difference between the settings for each reverb. In fact each of the 3 reverbs is for the most part, specially configured to operate with a range of values unique for just that reverb.

Now when I'm mixing I'm always thinking in terms of blend and contrast.

These are the two fundamental forces at play. Every mix is a balance of instruments that are blending together and instruments that are contrasting.

When instruments blend, they tend to fall towards the back of your mix. Anything that contrasts by its very nature will be pushing out from a background of blended instruments-- this is just how contrast works.

By default, without any mixing, instruments will blend together. Contrast is an artificial result achieved primarily through EQing and Reverb. Once you've made your EQ moves to create blend/contrast then the next most effective way to create more blend and contrast in your mix is through the use of reverb.

The reason I want you to understand blend and contrast is because the 3 regions of our mix—the **Front**, **Middle** and **Back** will be relying on the principles of blend and contrast in order for them to work. If they aren't set up to achieve some combination of blend and contrast then 3-Space Mix theory falls apart.

So in the next section we're going to go much deeper into blend and contrast and how it relates to reverb.

Paradigm #2: Blend/Contrast Theory and Reverb

Blend and contrast really is the most important mixing principle to follow.

What's really cool about reverbs is they tend to naturally blend together. This means you don't actually have to worry about different reverbs not blending together to create your desired environment.

So just remember that the sound of different reverbs will always merge together in some way.

The trick with reverb is how to go about creating contrast, because the more you can create contrast between reverbs the more depth you can create in your mix. Getting reverb spaces to contrast literally pushes reverbs apart, which creates more room for each reverb to articulate.

Now the way we'll be creating more contrast with reverbs is by having numerically different settings between the 3 main reverbs we will be using.

So a quick summary about blend/contrast with reverbs:

1. Reverbs by default will blend together.

2. To create more contrast with reverbs we use numerically different settings between each reverb.

The more similar the settings between two reverbs the more they will blend together. The more different they are, the more they push apart. The trick is knowing exactly where to make reverb settings different so it creates more depth (contrast). That's what this book is about.

Now before we get into the actual settings we'll be using for our 3 reverb types, we need to give you a rundown of the individual parameters. If you already feel comfortable with these then feel free to skip the next section.

Reverb Controls Explained

The most important parameters in any reverb are **pre-delay, decay and hi-cut**. The reason these 3 parameters are the most important is because all reverb plugins already have the presets arranged by the type of spaces they create. This allows us to flip through presets and find the general room we're after and simply adjust these 3 main parameters to quickly get the sound we're after.

Now the type of room a reverb simulates can be arranged into categories. These categories are the way in which all reverb presets are organized. Some presets are for small rooms and some are for halls, so they're organized in a way that makes it easy for you to find what you're looking for.

These categories are important because they will be used to create the Front, Middle and Back spaces of your mix.

The following is going to be a list of these reverb categories and which of the 3 spaces of our mix they help us accomplish.

Front Space Categories:

Drums, Small Rooms, Studios, Chambers

Middle Space Categories:
Chambers, Halls, Medium Rooms, Studios

Back Space Categories:
Chambers, Halls, Cathedrals

Now once you've got a space selected from one of these preset categories, all you'll generally need to adjust is the pre-delay, decay and hi-cut. These 3 parameters are your big movers. They will allow you to achieve 80% of the reverb result you're after.

But in case you want to go a little deeper, let's explain the reverb controls.

Mix

Tells you how much of the reverb effect is mixed in with the dry unaffected sound. The higher you turn up the mix knob the less you will hear the dry signal and the more you will hear the reverb. With mix at 100% you will only hear the reverb effect.

When using the reverb on a send always leave the mix at 100%.

Decay

Is how long it takes for the reverb to fade out after a source is fed into it. With a 2 second decay, when a source is fed into the reverb it will take 2 seconds for the sound of the reverb to fade out. The longer the decay the bigger the room is perceived.

Hi-cut

Is how much of the high frequency content you want to hear within the reverb. The more high frequencies you have in a room, the more up front it feels.

Typically drum rooms are the brightest sounding which means they have the most high frequency content, and that means leaving the hi-cut relatively open.

Pre-delay

Is how long it takes for us to actually hear the reverb once a sound is fed into it.

The most important aspect of pre-delay is that it allows us to separate the original source from the reverb effect which prevents unnecessary blending of the original source with the reverb. This is achieved with pre-delays of 3ms - 20ms.

Pre delay allows us to maintain clarity of the sound source by separating the reverb from the source by a small amount. It's very common on drum sounds to add 3 - 10ms of pre-delay just to give the drums more room to articulate; otherwise they could get smeared by the instantaneous merging of the reverb with the original drum sound.

On a technical level, pre-delay is the distance of your sound from the walls of the room you're trying to simulate.

The bigger the room, the larger the distance between your sound source and the walls of that room. As such longer pre-delays give us the impression of larger rooms.

This is the other parameter we use to determine the size of a room.

However, I will strongly state that I primarily rely on this parameter to rhythmically time my reverbs to taste instead of simulating room size, since decay is more reliable for that.

The essential takeaway is that as an example, the further a vocalist is from the nearest wall, the more predelay you get.

Pre-delay is like yelling in a large valley and the time it takes for you to hear your 1st echo come back to you. As the echo decays throughout the valley eventually it washes into a sort of reverberant sound. This is much more accelerated and pronounced in cathedral or large halls; it's also a lot more musical, which is why reverbs are generally simulating closed rooms instead of open valleys.

Large pre-delays give us the impression of larger spaces since only large spaces can have large pre-delays.

I honestly didn't want to give you the technical explanation, because I think it's more important to set your pre-delay creatively in terms of what sounds are going into it and how you want it to respond to those sounds. The choice is yours.

The safest predelays are 3 - 20ms. You really can't go wrong with predelay in this range.

One other thing to be aware is that the back space will almost always have a considerably short predelay, generally less than 10ms.

This is because if it has a short predelay then it means its right next to a wall in the back space of your mix. The rule goes that if it's against the back space's wall in our imaginary space, then it must have a short pre-delay.

If it's far away from our back wall then it has a larger predelay and that by default means it's in the front of the room. Your lead elements will almost always have the largest predelay, which not only makes them sound livelier, but also brings them forward in your mix. This is why pre-delay is so useful.

Size

Is the size of the room being simulated. Size controls the spacing of the initial echoes in the room you're trying to simulate.

When you make a sound in any room, initially there are a few separate echoes from the sound 1st bouncing off each wall and back to you. But then the echoes keep bouncing back and forth, multiplying and diffusing and this creates the characteristically diffuse and washed sound of reverb.

So reverb is actually the result of echoes multiplying so fast in a room that they smear and blend together which creates that pleasing washed sound that reverbs are known for.

Size allows us to control the spacing of our initial echoes, such that the larger the echo spacing the larger our perception of the room. Since larger rooms have more spaced echoes it means that smaller rooms will have little or almost no space between echoes.

Whenever I'm increasing the size parameter I'm doing it to increase the spacing between echoes in a given room. This is because the more spaced the echoes are the larger my perception of it.

The truth is that size and decay work together to give us our overall perception of size.

I often use size to give the sense of a larger room when I don't want to have the decay so long that it conflicts with other long reverbs. The benefit is that I can create the feel of a large room, but use a shorter decay time.

You might at this point be noticing some overlap between parameters like predelay, decay and size when trying to simulate the size of a space. I'll get rid of any confusion by saying that these overlap because they can all work independently to influence our perception of size.

What that means is that any one of them in isolation can be used by your brain to determine the size of a space. What's really cool about that is that you don't actually have to follow scientific rules which state that a larger space will always have a longer decay, longer predelay, and more spaced initial echoes (size).

All you have to do is just set one of these controls so it's perceived as a larger (or smaller) space and the brain will take care of the rest. Because of this you really can't go wrong when configuring reverb. There is in fact no wrong way to configure a reverb as long as you follow the rules I'll be giving you. Just remember that the most important parameter for determining size really is the length of your decay.

Diffusion

Is related to the size parameter. As you'll remember the size parameter increases the distance between the initial echoes generated by the reverb.

What diffusion does is 'wash' those echoes, which means it blurs them.

Diffusion is the difference between hard stone walls and walls covered with books and other objects. Because of the many uneven surfaces on walls covered with books, when a sound wave hits it, the wave is dispersed in many different directions, thus making it difficult to perceive the individual echo.

A super duper awesome Snapple ™ fact is that this is the same idea behind stealth jets. Radar is a waveform and if you want to avoid it you diffuse it in many different directions.

If you've increased the size parameter in your reverb but feel the echoes are too detectable, diffusion allows you to blend the echoes into the reverb so they sound more natural.

Mod Depth

Is the depth of pitch modulation happening within your reverb.

It's basically like chorusing on your reverb, which allows you to make it sound smoother and less digital sounding. Whereas actual chorusing can be very audible and cause phasing, mod depth will simply modulate the pitch of the reverb in a way that is much more musical and less unnatural than a chorus effect.

In terms of blend and contrast between the 3 spaces of my mix. The front space typically has the least amount of mod depth, the middle is in between and the back has the most amount of pitch modulation happening.

You don't have to follow this rule to get a great mix, but I generally find it really helpful for configuring the middle and back spaces because reverbs that are very long sound delicious with some chorusing whereas the more up front middle space sounds a bit more lively and in your face with less chorusing.

Mod Rate

Is how fast the pitch modulation moves up and down. The faster it is the more it becomes like vibrato. I almost always keep this at 1.1khz or less.

Some rules of thumb to follow when tweaking mod rate with mod depth:

1. The higher the mod rate, the less mod depth you can have for the reverb to sound natural.

2. The lower the mod rate, the more mod depth you can have for the reverb to sound natural.

Those are just rules, but remember mod rate and mod depth is just about adding gentle and natural pitch modulation to your reverb to give it a little more life and prevent it from sounding digital.

EQ Decay (Multiplier)

I call this the EQ Decay Multiplier, but it's often labeled things like bass/high frequency multipliers and in one particular intuitive reverb they are called darkness/brightness controls.

Darkness/brightness of the reverb is probably the best label for what the EQ Decay Multiplier controls are designed to achieve:

1. A darker reverb will have bass frequencies that last longer relative to the high frequencies.

2. A brighter reverb will have bass frequencies which decay faster relative to high frequencies.

Going after Darkness/Brightness should be the only reason you'll be looking at these controls. After configuring your decay and high cut settings, if those aren't enough, you can then ask yourself, "Do I want a brighter or darker room?"

If you want a darker room then make sure the high frequency content decays faster (than your bass frequency content).

If you want a brighter room, then make sure the low frequency content decays faster (than your high frequency content).

I have a really set and forget way of configuring these. I've just generally found that having the bass frequency crossover at 1khz works really well. The multiplier configuration is up to you.

For the high frequency multiplier I've found that having the crossover in the 5khz range works really well for most of my applications.

I determined these numbers by working with a lot of reverbs over the years and noticing that the best and most versatile presets were often configured in this fashion.

If there's a pattern I'll take it and use it. As an artist I already waste enough time trying to be creative and make my own patterns so there's no reason I can't benefit from somebody else's work—it saves me time.

The reason I call it EQ Decay is because that's what they actually do. These controls allow us to control the decay time of individual frequency bands within our reverb.

With the 1khz bass and 5khz high frequency crossovers I've suggested above it means that you're able to control how fast the bass frequencies and high frequencies decay in the most musical way possible.

Now EQ Decay settings can be use not only for brightening/darkening a sound, but also as an EQ to shape the balance of a reverb.

As a quick example I'll often want the bass frequencies in my **Front Space (short-decay reverb)** to decay faster because it sounds cleaner and leaves more space for everything else in my mix. So what I'll do is set my bass multiplier so that its value is lower than my high frequency multiplier. This causes the bass frequencies to disappear much faster than the high frequencies which makes the reverb less bass heavy and thus creates more room for bass frequencies in my mix.

This is just like EQing, only it is frequency and time dependent as opposed to static and always happening by the same amount.

EQ Hicut and Lowcut

Is just a regular EQ for shaping the tonal balance of your reverb. It's one of the most important controls for mixing reverb.

I personally rely on this more for shaping the tone of my reverb than I do the EQ decay multiplier. I always try to get away with it 1st simply because it's the easiest and I like doing things the easy way.

Since I almost always use reverb on sends. I prefer to simply follow the reverb with a separate EQ, that way I can Locut and Hicut as well as use bell shaped boosts/cuts. Most EQ's within reverbs aren't flexible this way.

The 3 Reverb Types Explained

As we've already discussed, I divide the space of a mix into 3 regions. They are the **Front, Middle and Back spaces**. I used movie theatre rows to illustrate this, but as an artist you can imagine any space you want for this to work.

As you'll remember, the 3 reverbs types are short-decay, medium-decay and long-decay reverbs. Each reverb type is designed to create the perception of the front, middle and back spaces of your mix.

So put simply you have:

The **front space** is created by using **short-decay reverbs**. Short-decay reverbs are often referred to as small rooms.

The **middle space** is created by using **medium-decay reverbs**. Medium-decay reverbs are often referred to as medium rooms.

The **back space** is created by using **long-decay reverbs**. Long-decay reverbs are often referred to as large/hall rooms.

So now that we've learned enough about short, medium, and long-decay reverbs let's talk in depth about their decay settings.

We are beginning with the decay settings because this is the first point of contrast between your reverb spaces and what allows them to create the perception of depth between the front, middle and back spaces of your mix.
If your reverb spaces fail to have contrasting settings with their decays then you'll lose a lot of depth and clarity in your mix.

Short-Decay Reverb
(Front Space)
Has .1 - 1sec of decay

To me it's the sound of a bathroom or a really nice drum studio. It's the brightest sounding reverb in your mix, meaning it has the least high frequency roll off happening.

The idea is that it's the shortest reverb in your mix and is typically best suited for your drums. I generally name this my Drum Verb, even though I give myself permission to send other instruments to it if I feel the need to.

We use the short-decay reverb to create the **Front space** of our mix.

Medium-Decay Reverb
(Middle Space)
Has 1 - 2.5 seconds of decay

To me it's the sound of a somewhat larger and pleasant sounding garage or empty dance club.

It's the 2nd brightest sounding reverb in your mix, only behind your short-decay reverb. This means its hicut setting will allow more hi frequency content through than your long-decay reverb. Typically I set my hi cut on my medium-decay around 8 - 15khz

Because it's a bigger room it can have somewhat distinct echoes and so it generally has the most in your face sound of all the reverbs in your mix. It's best for leads, vocals, and anything you want up front in your mix.

Notice I said up front, it's probably now I should make the distinction that even though you'll setup a Front Space Reverb that it's actually the middle space reverb which will be responsible for giving listeners the sense of magnitude you'd want the front/middle spaces of your mix to have.

That may be a bit confusing to understand at first, but this will clear it up:

1. We use the medium-decay reverb to create the **middle space** by making sure we generously send instrument signals to it

2. If we sparingly apply the middle space reverb to instruments then it tends to keep them in the front of the mix, assuming those instruments are loud enough already. That's because loud stuff sounds close, and quiet stuff sounds far. If it's loud and up close in real life you perceive room characteristics less because it's the source of the noise that is important to your brain.

The **middle space** reverb overlaps with the **front space** reverb simply because of it's in your face sound, as well as its longer decay which is what makes it more detectable. Add to the fact that you'll be sending leads to it, and this is why it has the effect of occupying the front space by the sheer importance of the instruments going into it.

Long-Decay Reverb
(Back Space Reverb)
Has 2.5 – 8 seconds of decay

To me it's the sound of a large stone walled church/cathedral. It has an epic quality to it. We use this reverb to create the furthest regions of your mix and it achieves this by way of having the longest decay.

As you'll remember, the farther something is away from us, the longer the decay we expect it to have.

The long-decay reverb is the longest mixing purpose reverb in your mix. I say longest mixing purpose reverb because within this framework the Front, Middle and Back Space reverbs will be your primary reverbs for sending instruments to.

Now there's actually a 4th type of reverb but it isn't really a part of my 3-Space Reverb Framework.

The 4th type of reverb is an FX reverb. It really isn't so much an extra space as it is any number (beyond your core 3 reverbs) of <u>utility reverbs</u> you add for creative effect/mixing purposes.

I often want my FX to be in the same reverb as my back space or middle space reverbs. However for those particular reverbs they often have too long of decays for the FX that are going into them. I tend to prefer having slightly tighter reverbs (shorter decay settings) for FX, so I just take the back or middle reverbs and copy them over to an FX send and simply shorten the decay.

<u>FX-Decay Reverb</u>
(Utility Reverb)
Any length of decay

I call these utility reverbs, because they function outside your core 3 Reverbs. Just keep in mind that these reverbs are meant to support your 3 main reverbs in ways they couldn't accomplish.

The idea is that this reverb is your wildcard reverb and it can have unusual decay or pre-delay settings (or completely different settings altogether).

Keep in mind that if 2 or more utility reverbs start having a substantial amount of really different settings from your core 3 reverbs you risk blurring the perception of the environment in your mixes. It doesn't mean you can't do this, because most people frankly won't notice, but when it comes time to do some deeper mixing you might notice some issues presented by getting a bit too messy with your reverbs.

The reason I use a separate reverb for FX is because FX are generally support elements that I want sitting in the back space of my track.

Unfortunately, if I send FX to my long-tail reverb they won't sound as tight, because they will incur a very long decay from the back reverb and thus eat up my precious mixing real-estate. If I send them to the middle reverb, they could swamp my leads. If I send them to the front reverb, they can sound too close.

That being said, I'm lazy and I always try to fit my FX into the Front, Middle or Back Reverbs before reaching for a 4th FX specific reverb. Often times this works just fine for me and it generally sounds more natural. However, some of the time I do need extra reverbs just for FX and other creative considerations.

My FX reverb typically has the decay settings of somewhere between my short-tail reverb and medium-tail reverb. So somewhere between 1 - 2.5 seconds of decay.

I find 1.5 seconds to be a golden number because it gives FX the feeling of space, while also making it so the reverb decay doesn't extend over the other spaces of my mix.

My mixes will typically have an additional number of utility reverbs as necessary. I do find that as the number of utility reverbs goes up beyond 2 that my mixes become a little more chaotic and require more precise configuration and handling of my reverbs. So it's just something to keep in mind that keeping it simple really does have musical benefits.

The 3-Space Reverb Framework

Setting up reverb to be used in a project is fairly straight forward. There are generally two options. One is to set up 3 reverbs before you start doing anything. The other is to set them up as you go.

I prefer having the 3 reverbs configured in a template before I open my project so that I can get right into the production process. This doesn't mean that I don't configure my reverbs once I'm in the creative process—it's just a way to help me to get right into making music.

The goal with using this framework is to create 3 spaces in your mix that contrast in such a way as to increase the perceived depth of your mix whenever instruments are fed into them.

So let's show you how to set them up.

The Front Space Reverb

(Short-Decay)
Preset Categories:
Drums, Small Rooms, Plates and Chambers

Predelay: 1 - 10ms

Decay: .2 – 1 sec

Hicut: 10k - 20k

Diffusion: To taste. Low diffusion create a more lively, and echoey drum room. High diffusion creates a smoother drum room.

Mod Rate/Depth: Mod depth is somewhere between 5 - 20%.

Remember that with lower mod depths you can use higher mod rates.

Will typically have the least modulation depth happening.

EQ: A drum room's low frequencies should disappear before its high frequencies

The Middle Space Reverb
(Medium-Decay)
Preset Categories:
Halls, Chambers and Studios

Predelay: 10 - 20ms

Decay: 1 – 2 sec

Hicut: 8k - 15k

Diffusion: Set to taste.

Remember Low diffusion creates a more lively room. Beware that with leads, low diffusion settings can cause flutter echoes which can smear the clarity of the source.

Mod Rate/Depth: Mod depth is typically somewhere between 5 – 30%.

Remember that with lower mod depths you can have higher mod rates.

Very experimental with this space, but typically it has a lower mod rate and depth than your back space because if the modulation is too heavy then it pushes this space toward the back of your mix.

EQ: This medium-decay reverb's EQ settings are configured so that they complement your long-decay reverb's EQ in such a way that they give each other space.

As an example if your long-decay (back space) reverb has a lot of bass content as it decays, you'll want your medium-tail to be a little less bass heavy as it decays. Whether you EQ those frequencies out or do it with the EQ Decay Multiplier is up to you.

The Back Space Reverb
(Long-Decay)
Preset Categories:
Halls, Chambers and Cathedrals

Predelay: 1 - 15ms.

We can simulate things being in the back of your mix when the space not only has a long decay but also when the predelay is somewhat short (<10ms). This is because stuff in the back of your mix would be the closest to the wall which means there's very little predelay.

Decay: 2 – 8sec

Hicut: 5k - 12k

Of your 3 reverbs this will have the most amount of hicut happening. This not only pushes it further in the back of your mix but also creates more contrast between the middle and back spaces.

Diffusion: Virtually always at max.

You don't want to hear any flutter echoes in a back space because it's simulating the largest space in your mix.

Mod Rate/Depth: Mod Depth is typically somewhere between 15 - 50%.

1.1khz mod rate really is an excellent starting place for any reverb. I can't stress enough how often I end up around this number for my mod rate.

Remember with higher mod depths that you'll usually want a lower mod rate; otherwise your pitch becomes very obviously wobbly.

EQ: Typically has the most natural bass decay which means that if your decay is 2 seconds long then your bass multiplier will be anywhere from .90 to 1.5.

What gives the back space its perceived epicness/largeness is the fact that the bass decay is longer than your other reverbs.

How to EQ Reverb

Reverb is meant to create a sense of space, but at the same time it's meant to do so without overtaking the instruments populating it.

If you enjoy using lots of reverb then at some point or another you'll run into the issue of reverb overwhelming your mix. This typically happens during choruses as more and more instruments start simultaneously feeding into your reverbs.

While there are lots of ways to avoid this, often times it's just a side effect of many instruments being sent to the same reverb. You could decrease the sends, but very often you'll have your reverbs populating your mix just the way you want it.

This is where EQ comes in.

EQ allows you to shape the frequency density of your reverb so that it supports your instrumentation rather than overtakes it.

By relying on simple hicuts and low cuts coupled with peak cuts/boosts we can shape our reverb to better support our mix goals. What's really cool about this technique is that in the context of a mix, nobody is going to notice the difference.

While you'll usually be subtracting reverb with this technique, the end result will actually be an increase in the perceived depth and expansiveness of your mix.

The good news is that EQing reverb is incredibly straight forward. We'll go through each of the spaces and talk about how to EQ them separately so as to allow them to work together as naturally as possible.

Front Space EQ Settings

Low frequencies (<100hz):
Always lowcut at 120hz with 12 - 24db/oct filter. Reverbs generating content at sub 100hz frequencies just muddies up your mix.

I should say that with the Front Space I sometimes make use of an aggressive 6 or 12db/oct lowcut that is somewhere around 500hz. This allows me to get all the ambience qualities of the reverb and to be able to feed it hard without over-populating those precious <500hz frequencies of my mix.

But to start things off I always leave a regular low cut at 120hz. As my mixes progress I might decide I need more space in these low frequencies so I might escalate the cut to somewhere around 500hz.

When engineers/producers have too much clashing in the <500hz frequency range they get the symptom of a muddy and undefined mixes. This is one of a multitude of steps for curing for that problem.

Mid Frequencies (100hz - 5khz):
It's entirely up to you what you do here. You generally shouldn't need to EQ the mid frequencies of this reverb because its decay is so short. But if you feel it's too dense in this region then go ahead. Use wide, gentle 1-3db dips.

Hi Frequencies (5khz - 20khz):
Since the front space is also my drum room it generally sounds better to have the 10khz - 15khz frequencies coming through. This makes it play more forward and its short decay/duration means the high frequencies can play full force without impinging on the rest of the mix.

I like my drum room to sound bright, so allowing these to come through gives it that good vibe. The most important thing to remember is that hi cutting your drum room is dependent on the mix, if it's too bright relative to everything else, then you hicut to smooth it out.

There's nothing wrong with cutting top frequencies down to 5khz, because sometimes you just want to hear the room, but you don't want to hear it sizzle in your mix.

Keep in mind that the sizzle of a drum is what gives it its liveliness. That liveliness comes from those 10khz + frequencies. Cut these if you want to remove that. I deliberately rely on the sizzle of my drum room to allow it to excellently mix drums. You have to try it to believe it--sizzle is great on drum reverbs. It's about the only place it is good actually.

Plate style reverbs are generally known for their ability to sizzle

Middle Space EQ Settings

Low Frequencies (<150hz):
Low cut at 120 - 150hz with 12-24db/oct filters. You'll notice we're cutting a little more aggressively; this prevents our middle space from overtaking the rest of our mix.

Mid Frequencies (150hz - 5khz):
Again this is up to taste. I generally don't alter this range very much if at all.

When I do alter this range, 80% of the time I'm doing a very wide .5db - 2db dip around 1khz to prevent the reverb from swamping the midrange intelligibility of my lead instruments which occupy this range. This is one of my favorite EQ moves to clean up the middle space of my mix.

High Frequencies (5khz – 20khz):
Since this reverb is actually most responsible for populating the front space of my mix, I generally don't remove much of the high frequencies.

To maintain its liveliness I prefer using hi shelving filters to darken it a little if necessary. If I use a hicut it is typically happening around 8 - 15khz with a 12db/oct filter.

Keep in mind that I'm telling you my preferences; it's up to you to experiment and find what you like most. Always trust your intuitions.

Back Space EQ Settings

Low Frequencies (<150hz):

We low cut the same as the middle space. We are low cutting frequencies 150hz and lower with a 12 – 24db/oct filter. We just don't need these and it cleans up the low end of our mix.

Mid Frequencies (150hz - 5khz):

It's same as the medium tail. I generally don't alter it very much, but if it's aggressively populated by many instruments I'll sometimes do a wide .5db - 2db dip around 1khz to clean up the mid range and improve intelligibility.

Hi Frequencies (5khz – 20khz):

I'm virtually always hicutting my long-tail reverb around 5k - 10khz with a 12db/oct filter, sometimes even a 6db/oct if I need something gentler. Your reverb's included hi and lowcut parameters should be sufficient for this.

By cutting the high frequencies we're pushing the back space even further back in our mix. This allows us to create a deliberate point of contrast between the more high frequency rich middle-space reverb and our darker back space reverb.

Also since it's usually so long in decay, hicutting not only helps clean up the high frequency real-estate of your mix, but it also contributes to the natural perception of this reverb space being the furthest, since sounds which are furthest away have the most high frequency roll off.

Something to keep in mind when EQing reverb, is that you don't want to dramatically change the shape of the reverb with an EQ. That means excessively deep cuts or boosts can risk sounding unnatural and negatively impact the fidelity of your reverb.

As a rule of thumb you want to avoid doing any aggressive cuts or boosts to 150hz - 5khz as this could render the reverb obsolete in terms of intelligibility.

If you feel the need to do these kinds of deep cuts or boosts, then you should be relying on the EQ Decay Multipliers so you can get the aggressive frequency balance that you want.

The exception to the rule of not doing deep cuts/boosts is when aggressively low cutting a reverb being specifically used to add ambience. This is most commonly done on the Front Space Reverb. The low cut will often land somewhere around 500hz. This allows the reverb to do its spatial magic by populating the higher frequencies with reverb information without taking up that precious sub 500hz real-estate.

Advanced Reverb Techniques

These are more advanced techniques for reverb. I would suggest holding off on them until you're at least a little comfortable using the 3-space reverb framework I presented earlier.

Multiband Compressing Reverb

When I talk about multiband compressing reverb I mean sending every reverb in your mix to a single group. In that group you then set up a multiband compressor to selectively reduce the volume of any given frequency range as it gets too loud.

This is also known as dynamic EQing. It's just like EQing reverb, only it has the added benefit of allowing us to selectively reduce the volume of a given frequency range whenever it becomes too loud with reverb energy.

It's important to control reverb volume in a given frequency range because sometimes while everything in your mix is feeding into your reverb, it can cause the overall amount of reverb happening to overwhelm your mix.

So what we'll be doing is using multiband compression to limit the intensity of our reverb in a given frequency range.

The reason this is better than a regular EQ is because of the following. An EQ dip at 1khz for 2db would always reduce the energy in that range by 2db, no matter how quiet it becomes. A multiband compressor can be set so that 1khz only gets reduced by 2db when its loudness reaches a certain level.

I often find that the 700hz - 5khz range of reverbs can become overwhelming. So I like to set a multiband compressor to just shave off 1 - 2db in that range during just the dense (chorus) parts of my mixes.

It saves me a lot of time because I don't have to automate reverbs to keep them properly mixed—I can just lazy fix it with a multiband compressor.
Keep in mind that anything with more than 2db of gain reduction and too fast an attack and release risks creating unnatural pumping in your reverb. I'll show you how to do this properly in the next example.

Configuring Multiband Compression for Reverb

1. Grab any multiband compressor.

2. Disable all the other bands except for a middle band.
3. Setup the range of the middle band from 700hz - 5khz.
4. Set Attack to 30 - 50ms.
5. Set Release to 50 - 100ms.
6. Set Ratio 1.5:1.
7. Play a dense part of your track where all the reverbs are being used and bring the Threshold down until you hear a gentle spacing created by the reduction of the reverb density in that range. I typically like the sound of 1 - 2db of gain reduction

In this way we are using the multiband compressor as what's called a dynamic EQ which is really just an EQ that isn't static but instead reactively reduces the volume of a given frequency depending on how much energy is in that range.

When compressing reverb in this way it's important to realize that heavily compressing a frequency band will drastically alter the natural characteristics of the reverb. This means that care must be taken to make sure the gain reduction is happening as little and as naturally as possible.

Another thing to note is that the more instruments there are feeding into your reverbs at any given moment the less detectable this technique becomes. If however the track is very sparse and you go for 3db+ of gain reduction in the 700hz - 5khz range, it will have a fairly obvious effect on the openness of your track.

The Pre-Verb EQ

In most situations you'll be EQing after reverb, but I wanted to talk about the benefit of placing an EQ before a reverb.

Keep in mind that if you aren't sure what to do then always place EQ after reverb. I'm just giving you another technique you may find useful.

The idea of placing an EQ before a reverb to cut low frequencies is that for some reason I've always felt that even though you may have a signal at 100hz going into a reverb, it somehow causes the reverb to oscillate and generate added reverb content higher than 100hz.

Sometimes I don't want this added frequency content coming from the reverb so I often find that with reverbs that have a lot of bass instrumentation feeding into them, I prefer placing a low cut filter before the reverb.

This to me sounds cleaner for any reverb being fed by a lot of low frequency content. If your reverb isn't receiving that much bass frequency content then you can simply rely on placing the EQ after the reverb.

Mid/Side EQing For Reverb Width

One really simple and cool technique for giving reverb more perceived width is to use what we call mid/side EQing. I would suggest only using this technique once you're about to finish your mix.

Mid/side EQing has an absurd technical explanation behind it, but put simply the mid is the mono information of your signal, and the side is the stereo information of your signal. When they combine together you get the full signal.

What's cool about mid/side processing is we can use it to enhance the perceived width of a reverb while also cleaning up some space in the middle of our mix to allow our leads to sit more comfortably.

The way we do this is by setting up a side band shelving filter at 5khz+ boosting 1-2db.

You can also set a shelving filter @5khz+ subtracting 1-2db for just the mid signal.

This has the effect of clearing a little space for the instruments in the center of your mix while also adding some very gentle stereo width to your mix. Despite the fact that I would have considered this a big no no in the past I can tell you why it works.

Subtracting a little from the mid signal works because it gives your instrumentation in the middle of your mix more space to breathe. At the same time the added width of your side boost increases the overall stereo image of your mix in a very transparent way. These two forces happening together adds a very nice finishing touch to your tracks.

It's very similar to using a side-band low cut filter as the first insert of your master to remove frequencies 150hz and lower. The result of that technique is that you actually clean up the stereo intelligibility of your mix, thus improving its width because we generally want <150hz information to be focused in the center (mono) of our mix. It just sounds cleaner this way.

<u>Delay + Reverb</u>

Whether we send delay into reverb has always been a hot topic. I personally find that I'm almost always sending my delays into reverb because it sounds more natural.

The majority of synthesizer presets are setup this way and it sounds great. That being said, I do experiment with dry delays if I want my delay deliberately forward in my mix. Of all the sounds in your mix, the dry ones, if you decide to have them will sound the most forward and this can be sparingly used to create intense and unique front to back separation.

Blend/Contrasting Different Reverb Plugins

Different reverb plugins have different sounds. Because of this we can use two different reverb plugins to automatically create more contrast between the **Front** and **Back** spaces of our mix.

For the **Front Space** of my mixes I almost always enjoy using a bright/grainy reverb. This is the case because the front space is essentially our drum room reverb. A plate reverb generally works really well for this.

For the **Middle Space** of our mix, which as you know is mostly responsible for populating the front and middle regions of our mix I like to use a slightly grainy but still clear reverb. Most of the time I just use a more aggressive preset from one of my digital reverbs like Valhalla room.

For the **Back Space** of the mix I prefer using a very smooth and digital reverb because pristine and clear sounds naturally fall to the back of mixes. This is one of the benefits of using a digital reverb like Valhalla Room, Arts Acoustic or Aether.

The main idea here is to experiment with using a different reverb for the **Back Space** than you do for the **Front Space** of your mix.

So just remember that:
1. Clean/Digital Reverbs sit nicely in back
2. Grainy/Analog reverbs will tend to draw attention and so sit in the front.

Having these two types of reverb for the **Front** and **Back Spaces** will blow your mixes wide open. Since I know it's difficult to find the best reverb's out there, you can find my top 3 favorite reverbs in my personal plugin list included at the end of this book. I went through 500 or so plugins in the 8 years I've been producing/engineering and that list contains 20 of the 40 plugins that deserved to stay. I wasted a lot of time toying with plugins so hopefully that list will save you time.

The Mastering Reverb

Adding the same reverb to everything in your mix is the ultimate glue technique. If you aren't already then once you start doing this your mixes will hit a new level that you simply couldn't imagine.

Pros will occasionally mention they do this, but they often don't talk about how substantially it brings everything together in your mix. Put simply, it's better than bus compression at gluing things together, and bus compression is literally referred to as 'the glue.'

The trick with using reverb on your master is to create what I call a premaster reverb track and to then route every instrument/fx/send (everything) through this track. The premaster reverb track is then routed directly to your master. You will then create a separate Master Reverb Send where your master reverb goes. This master reverb send is routed directly to your master.

You will then use the premaster reverb track to send a small portion of the its signal to your master reverb send. The Master Reverb should be using a small room preset with .3 - .7sec of decay. You'll want to low-cut frequencies (<200hz) on your master reverb because you just won't need those, otherwise they will swamp your mix.

From the premaster track you can control how much all the instruments in your track are feeding this final reverb. The idea is to feed the master verb somewhat lightly so that it's almost imperceptible, but you can get fairly aggressive with this and that is very enjoyable to do as well.

This final reverb is meant to emulate the room your track is playing in. Like if you were playing your track through speakers in a club, this is what the master reverb is emulating, albeit with a much shorter decay. I don't know why, but it really makes a song come together in the most simply, impressive way.

This master reverb treatment happens pre-master, hence the pre-master reverb track we used. This does mean that I like running the Master Reverb + everything else in my session through my entire master treatment chain. There's nothing wrong with this for me because I don't rely too much on extreme forms of mastering for my projects.

That being said, one of the symptoms of heavy loudness maximization on your master is that the stereo width/ intelligibility of your track tends to go down. This can be remedied by configuring a master reverb on your project right before your final limiter.

This is just me getting into mix-engineer porn at this point, but the idea would be doing your entire master chain, except for your final limiter on a **'pre-master treatment track.'** You then send a little bit of your 'premaster treatment track' signal to your master reverb send, and then mix these all together at your Master right before the limiter.

This allows our master reverb to be unaffected by your mastering chain. What's really cool is that the heavy-handed effects of your pre-master treatment will influence the sounds going into your master reverb and all this is happening without the master chain negatively impacting your master reverb's stereo information and acoustics.

This is powerful because reverb information suffers the most from heavy compression and limiting. It's also an advanced technique that underlines the best mastering technique, namely that all really good mastering is a means of hiding the side-effects of mastering.

It works to hide mastering because while everything was heavily processed in your pre-mastering chain you're restoring some naturalness to it by running it through a reverb after the fact. And that reverb is only running into a limiter before your track is mixed down. It's this sequence that acts to hide mastering artifacts like multiband compression/limiter pumping.

Adding and configuring my pre-master reverb is my favorite mixing technique to do once I've finished composing and arranging a track. I then do my mixdown with this reverb enabled. The reason for this is because the pre-master verb allows you to get away with very aggressive and subtractive forms of mixing that some might call 'sterile mixing'.

Sterile mixing is typically the first skill level a producer encounters as they become increasingly competent with EQ.

At this level a producer has mastered the essence of subtractive EQ and understands that subtracting is more important than boosting. Because of this they spend more time looking for what they can get rid of, and unfortunately make the mistake of getting rid of some of the organic frequency chaos which actually gives their track life.

That being said a mastering engineer would rather have a sterile clean mix than a muddy unclean mix. He can breathe life back into sterile clean mixes, but he can't polish a turd of a muddy mix. He can only try his best to hide it.

I've not yet made a habit of mixing into my premaster reverb, which means having it already turned on as I put together my track, but it's something I've been meaning to experiment with.

I imagine it would make the track feel a little more organic and lively, because everything has that roomy quality as it's being put together.

Often times when putting a track together the lack of initial FX can make a song feel pretty shallow. Having this reverb already on can alleviate that and lead to more inspiration.

The Holy Trinity of Reverb

I'm always looking for ways to spice up the production process. Even though I like to adhere to a somewhat strict formula, I understand the importance of variety and giving myself new environments to experiment with.

Your DAW will almost always look the same, eventually you won't be acquiring any shiny new plugins and your project template will basically hit its final form.

While these are great achievements, sometimes these and other patterns create a kind of insidious familiarity that leads to a feeling of "oh this again," and a subsequent dulling of your desire to compose. Basically we're talking about creative block.

I don't consider myself a musical prodigy. My desire to make music comes and goes and I've learned to accept that. That being said I do place a conscious time limit on how long I'll allow myself to go without making a full song.

I believe that music production/engineering is a skill and so it must be exercised.

I'm lucky enough to have gotten past however many hours it took to be able to not produce for a month or two and come back to the studio and in 2-3 days rip out a new track.

This ability to come back after such long breaks is because I keep a studio journal where I write down my techniques and strategies for music production.

Everything you've read in this book is written in that journal, because I can and I do forget. The 3-Space Reverb Framework is actually written in my notes as "The Holy Trinity of Reverbs."

Much like the "Mathew McConaughey Music Maker Method," it had a funky name which didn't mean much to anyone except me. That brings me to a point, because if you decide to use a studio journal then be as creative with your naming as you want to be with your music.

It's a powerful memory technique that the weirdness of the name doesn't hurt; in fact it only makes it easier for you to remember the actual technique itself. We only really forget plain things—it's the unusual stuff that lingers a lot longer.

In case you're wondering the "Mathew McConaughey Method" is just about having a beaming attitude where every decision while producing/engineering is viewed with an overwhelmingly, positive "Alriiiight.. **All-right**," which I think is a great attitude to have when putting together music.

It's because of my journal that I'm able to remember why reverb is one of the most important tools to master and how I've gone about mastering it.

Right out the gate, the two most important mix tools to master are EQ and Reverb, then compression and then delay. If you'd like to learn more about EQ and Compression and how to use them together then you can check out my book, *The EQ and Compression Formula.*

By using the 3-Space Reverb Framework that I've given you, you will be able to skip past the unnecessary learning curve associated with reverb and just start composing your track.

Remember that the idea behind reverb is to simulate a space. A classical orchestra only has one space, and that music sounds just fine to me.

Orchestras are not wasting time thinking about the acoustics in the spaces they play because it's already set up. They just focus on playing music and this is why I think it's so important to use the 3-Space Reverb Framework. It's designed to help you quickly get moving.

I hope you have discovered just how useful the techniques in this book are. Like any learning tool you can keep it nearby for reference as you explore your own unique ways of using reverb. Good luck!

<u>Additional Resources</u>

SEE FOLLOWING PAGES
FOR FREE PREVIEWS OF EACH BOOK

Books by the Author:

The EQ and Compression Formula: Learn the step by step way to use EQ and Compression together
<u>https://amzn.to/2FbCubN</u>

The Bus Compression Framework: The set and forget way to get an INSTANTLY professional sounding mix
<u>https://amzn.to/2wzixN1</u>

Mastering Multi-Band Compression: 17 step by step multiband compression techniques for getting flawless mixes
<u>https://amzn.to/2k9fMci</u>

Nathan's Top 20 Plugins

Includes 3 of my most <u>**Massive Engineering Secrets**</u> that I won't **REVEAL** anywhere else!

[See Page-90 for the Top 20 Plugins]

**Free Music Production/Audio Engineering
Resources**
http://www.mybeatlab.com/tutorials

Book Previews

The EQ and Compression Formula: Learn the step by step way to use EQ and Compression Together

Visit: https://amzn.to/2FbCubN

The Rule of 300

One of the most frustrating issues many producers encounter is a muddy or undefined low end in their mixes. Producers run into this problem because the instruments occupying the 20hz to 400hz frequency range of their mix are having a conflict catastrophe.

The reality is 20hz – 400hz is the most difficult frequency range for us to master because our hearing isn't as adapted to noticing details in it.

In order to avoid this temporary, but inherent weakness in our low end hearing there is one simple rule we can follow—The Rule of 300.

The rule of 300 states that if it isn't bass, kick or snare, then you must high pass those instruments at 300hz or higher.

The higher you can get away with the better for your mix.

This rule eliminates the main causes of a muddy mix because as you now know we run into this problem when our 20hz to 400hz range is swamped by too many competing instruments.

When professional mixers talk about balance they mean it as if there's a balance scale in front of you and so imagine on the one end there is something heavy, and the other has something light. And like a balance scale **you must be very selective about which instrument(s) are frequency 'heavy' and which ones are frequency 'light.'**

Balance just means that it sounds pleasing to you, but when mixers talk about balance they mean that you're decisive about which instruments get to be frequency dense and which one's get to be frequency light in a given frequency zone.

By following this rule your mixes will immediately start occupying the top 5% of mixes out there.

The Bus Compression Framework: The set and forget way to get an INSTANTLY professional sounding mix

Visit: https://amzn.to/2wzixN1

Why Do We Call It Pocket Compression? (Instead of Bus Compression)

The reason I call this pocket compression is because the compressor action creates an artificial pocket around instruments within a compression group. This artificial pocket has the characteristic of giving all those instruments similar dynamic behavior.

When I say dynamic similarity I mean that the volume of all the instruments in that group is changing in relation to our bus compressor being triggered.

Because any instrument or simultaneous playing of instruments within a group could trigger compressor action, it means that every instrument plays a part in the group's dynamic behavior which is the point of bus compression.

When I say "compressor behavior" I mean the increasing/decreasing of gain reduction. The rate and speed at which gain reduction increases/diminishes is the result of your attack and release settings.

It should be noted that within a bus compression group there's typically a few louder instruments that have a greater impact on the behavior of the compressor.

Other instruments are often too quiet to actually trigger or have a big influence on the compressors behavior. A good example of this would be in a drum bus.

In a drum bus the compressor movement is typically being driven by your kick and snare. Hi-hats don't generally trigger the compressor and this is because they usually aren't loud enough to do so.

Now with bus compression you're actually using a compressor to give instruments specific time-dependent volume characteristics. That's just a fancy way of saying you're making instruments within a group breathe relative to one another. As I've mentioned with my technique, this breathing/pumping is so subtle that it actually glues instruments together dynamically.

The dynamic glue we're talking about is this subtle rhythmic pumping/breathing. The rate and speed of the subtle pumping/breathing is the result of your attack and release settings.

The other glue effect we've already mentioned is simply the fact that all bus compressors impart a subtle and transparent form of saturation across all instruments running through them. This saturation simply adds harmonics to these instruments in about the same way in about the same place. This subtly unifies the "tone signature" of all our instruments which gives our mixes a professional sense of cohesion.

Now with my technique I simply use SSL bus compressors. They're perfect and there's a reason everyone loves them. This imparts the same saturation across all instruments no matter what group they're being sent to, thus gluing and unifying the tone of my entire mix.

Now with pocket compression we are deliberately forcing instruments to behave the same in relation to the compressor they're going into.

My favorite way to think about it is imagine you've got an elastic balloon around a group of instruments. The compressor settings determine how much space there is between the balloon edges and the instruments. This amount of space is the same thing as your Threshold setting.

At some point your instruments will get so loud that they fill in this extra space and begin to press against the edges of your balloon. How stretchy or not stretchy the balloon is is determined by your Ratio.

A 2:1 Ratio is the best stretchiness for this balloon, virtually always.

The rate and speed at which the balloon stretches when instruments get too loud and press into its edges is determined by your Attack and Release settings.

And so with bus compression you're limiting the volume freedom of instruments as if there was an elastic balloon being placed around them preventing them from moving too far beyond the initial boundaries of the balloon.

It's this artificial effect of creating an elastic boundary around instruments that is pocket compression.

This main idea is so simple, and amazingly powerful because it means that faster attacks (.1 - 3ms) and slower releases (.6 - 1sec) pushes stuff in the back of the mix, which creates **blend** and slower attacks (10 - 30ms) and fast releases (.1 - .3sec) allow grouped instruments to remain more open, dynamic and in front of the mix which creates **contrast**.

Mastering Multi-Band Compression: 17 step by step multiband compression techniques for getting flawless mixes

Visit: https://amzn.to/2k9fMci

Blend/Contrast Theory and Multiband Compression

If you've read any of my other books then you know that the foundation of my mixing philosophy is **blend** and **contrast**. I want for 70% of my instruments to blend together into the background of my mix, and the other 30% to contrast and push forward into the front of my mix.

By following this rule I'm able to create massive depth with less effort and less stress.

I can assure you, within a few sessions of applying this paradigm it will transform the way you approach mixing. You'll be more exacting with your decisions and you won't find yourself getting stuck debating whether something is right or wrong.

All you need to do is decide if an instrument is **blending** or **contrasting**.

At every level of my mixing, this is my primary goal. Why do I use *The 3-Space Reverb Framework* when mixing? Because it's sonically designed to create more **blend** and **contrast**.

Why do I rely on 4-Zone Mix theory in *The EQ and Compression Formula*? Because in each of the 4 frequency zones I always make sure there's 1 instrument that's louder (**contrasting**) and the rest are just supporting (**blending**).

How specifically am I using Bus Compression in *The Bus Compression Framework*? I'm using it to create improved blending via the 'glue' effect of compression. But I'm also applying deliberately, different compression settings to **blending** and **contrasting** instrument groups.

The different settings pushes blending and contrasting groups apart which creates more depth. As such a contrasting instrument group will always have more open compression settings compared to a blending instrument group which has slightly more restricted compression settings.

It's the additive effect of these precise and repeatable techniques which creates increasing levels of blend/contrast. With increasing levels of blend/contrast we can make massive depth and crystal clarity a virtually effortless byproduct of a formulaic mixing methodology.

This is what I aim for when I teach this stuff.

Can you make someone a great mixer right away? No, but you can teach them the exact sequences and patterns that great mixers use.

Unfortunately many great artists and mixers aren't exactly aware of how they do what they do and I think that's bullshit because it holds the rest of us back. It makes those of us just starting think the learning curve is steep.

It isn't as steep as we think. It's the initial time investment that's steep. But that's the price for anything worth having.

So everything I talk about is a formula. It's a methodology that you can copy and paste into your process to get an instant skip over the confusion.

We really need to experience results that we can appreciate in order to connect the deeper dots—the ones we're really after.

So knowing whether I'm after **blend** or **contrast** is my deeper connecting of the dots. It lets me know exactly what to do so that I don't get lost trying to figure out what I'm after. It's very simple and at the same time, this way of mixing isn't so rigid or encumbering that it drops me from a creative state.

Blend/contrast is a universal of art. Our perceptions are built around it. Hot-cold, black-white, happy-sad, quiet-loud, distant-close; everything.

So when we're mixing it's all about intensifying blend/contrast and the way we do this with multiband compression has to do with the 2 main results Multiband Compression can achieve. They are as follows:

1. **Transient Control**
    a. **Transient Enhancement**
    b. **Transient Reduction**
2. **Volume Leveling**

These 2 results also happen to be the exact same ways we use a regular compressor.

The only difference is that now we can do it on a specific frequency range which is what gives us the ability to use a multiband compressor to flexibly shape the frequency content of a sound.

Again, you can only shape a given frequency range if it has differences in volume to work with. If it's always sustaining at the same general volume, then multiband compression has virtually no positive benefit worth confusing ourselves with.

Transient Control for Blend/Contrast

Transient in the context of a multiband compressor means shaping the peak volume of a frequency range. Now the sentence I just said is true, but it can be super vague, so don't worry because the first 2 multiband compression techniques I'm going to give you will show you exactly how to achieve transient control.

For the most part it is going to be the results that connect the dots. The 17 techniques I'm going to be showing you a little later will give you the exact results you need to figure things out.

Examples are almost always clearer than the technical explanations. Technical explanations are just meant to prime your mind so that you're a little more subconsciously prepared to connect the dots when you get a demonstration later on.

So as a quick review here's exactly what I mean about transient control as it relates to **blend** vs. **contrast**:

1. **Transient Enhancement will always = More Contrast**
2. **Transient Reduction will always = More Blend**

Volume Leveling for Blend/Contrast

Volume leveling in the context of a multiband compressor means reducing the difference between loud and quiet portions of a given frequency range.

In our earlier example with the piano hammer playing louder and then quieter, we can set compression to reduce the volume of just the loud part so it gets closer in volume to the quiet part. Then simply applying makeup gain brings the overall level of volume back up, hence **volume leveling**.

Whenever a given frequency range gets too loud it begins to contrast and move toward the front of our mix. When it gets too quiet it can overly blend and eventually disappear into the background of our mix.

So we volume level frequency ranges because sometimes they're too loud and sometimes they're too quiet and leveling out the volume level makes that frequency range sit more stably in your mix.

Generally in mixes you want the majority of instruments to remain fairly dynamically stable because this gives you control over their mix placement.

But mixing is an art, and sometimes having 1 or 2 instruments be able to dynamically warp in and out of your mix because of their dramatic changes in volume can create more contrast and depth.

As you'll learn in the techniques I'm going to show you, much of the time we simply reduce the volume of loud parts without applying makeup gain. This is something that's counterintuitive because makeup gain is sort of presented as the final step of using any compressor and so some people assume it's meant to be used all the time—it's not, I'm going to show and explain why later on.

Volume Leveling is primarily a **blend** effect, simply because it holds stuff in place. But you can also hold stuff in place so it's louder and more present and in this way it becomes more of a **contrast effect.**

With volume leveling we are using the multiband compressor to prevent individual frequency ranges from darting back and forth throughout our mix.

You'll get a perfect example of **volume leveling** frequencies that move back and forth in your mix with technique #3. In that technique I'll show you the very visual example of how to control resonantly sweeping frequencies in your mix.

In fact, the reason volume leveling is so effective when dealing with sweeping resonances is because sometimes we like lots of resonance, but it can be overwhelming in certain frequency ranges and so wont fit perfectly with the mix. Volume leveling with multiband compression is the ultimate solution to this problem.

The techniques you're going to learn are the ones I use. Because it's me, they are incredibly formulaic and they work.

I'm giving them to you, partly because I feel obligated since I know I'm not the only one who was, for the longest time, ruthlessly tortured by multiband compression at a CIA blacksite called my studio.

I only want for you to find out for yourself just how effective the techniques are because they're going to free up a lot of mental energy so you can eventually focus on more important decisions like **blend** and **contrast**.

The more we don't have to think about **how** to use something and the more we can just fiddle with a tool while aiming for something simple like "**is it blending or contrasting?**" the more it becomes an enjoyable exploration and the more creativity blossoms.

<u>Nathan's Top 20 Plugins</u>

As a gift for reading this far I'm going to be revealing 3 of my biggest engineering secrets and the exact plugins I use to achieve them. This is the only place you'll ever find this stuff so give it a read and prepare to upgrade your mixes!

Aside from Verbsuite Classics I've consistently used each processor within this list for 3 – 8 years. I strongly believe in these tools.

I will only use plugins that sound great and which are efficient and easy to use. Simplicity and speed is crucial for consistently getting into a creative flow and so I only use tools which support that.

I already went through the 6 years of trying/owning 500+ plugins and trying out that many plugins was a big waste of time and only hindered my improvement.

It is my sincere hope that this list will save you the time I lost, because today I only have 40 or so plugins and these are the Top 20 I couldn't live without.

Digital EQ (Transparent EQ)

FabFilter Pro-Q 2

This is my workhorse EQ. I use it about 90% of the time. The other 10% is character EQing. It has an excellent graphical interface and is by far the easiest EQ to use. It's extremely transparent which means you won't hear it negatively affecting the sound. It contains essential mid/side processing as well as linear phase settings for use in mastering.

Visit: http://bit.ly/2Ip04rh

Analog EQ's (Character EQ's)

Virtual Mix Rack 2.0

Contains two Analog EQ's: FG-N and FG-S as well as an amazing compressor (FG-401) and 1176 Limiter. I classify these as "Character EQ's." I only use these EQ's for boosting because of their lush and vibrant boost-dependent saturation. Whereas a regular digital EQ like FabFilter Pro-Q 2 is going to transparently shape a sound, these EQ's will literally breathe life into dull and lifeless sources. You only need to hear the boosts to become a believer.

Visit: http://bit.ly/2jMqky7

Bus Compressors

Virtual Bus Compressors

Virtual Bus Compressors contains 3 of the most popular bus compressors emulations including an SSL Bus compressor (FG-Grey). Using these on a mix in the multi-layered way I teach in *The Bus Compression Framework* will kill any of the blandness inherent in digital recordings. The FG-Grey alone is worth the price tag, but you get 2 bonus legendary bus compressors. I really couldn't live without the FG-Grey because its saturation characteristics are 60 - 70% responsible for the professional signature of my sound.

Visit: http://bit.ly/2wvVHGk

Compressors

FabFilter Pro-C 2

This is the Swiss Army knife of compressors. It can do any kind of sound from smooth and transparent all the way to snappy and aggressive pumping. I use it for everything, especially if I'm unsure what compressor to use. With its easy to understand visual display it's the most noob friendly and educational compressor there is. If I had started with this compressor I probably would of learned how to use compression about 50% faster. It has deep sidechaining capabilities as well as multiple compressor styles making it's the best all around compressor. If I could only live with one compressor this would be it.

Visit: http://bit.ly/2FZfYnb

FG-401 (Part of Virtual Mix Rack 2.0)

My go to vocal compressor/LA-2A on steroids. It's capable of being extremely transparent and gentle on sounds while bathing them in a heavenly layer of saturation. You have the option of enabling/disabling the saturation stage of this compressor which is awesome. I use this as a transparent volume leveler/tone enrichment tool. I don't use it for enhancing transients or the body of sounds as I personally feel it's too gentle for this. I primarily use the FG 401 as more flexible and configurable LA-2A.

Visit: http://bit.ly/2jMqky7

De-Essers

FabFilter Pro-DS

For me personally I find this to be the easiest and most versatile De-Esser there is. I used the Waves De-Esser before this, but this one is significantly better sounding and more flexible. If you record vocals and you're sick of sibilance this is the cure.

Visit: http://bit.ly/2rv904W

Limiter

FabFilter Pro-L 2

This is my all around workhorse limiter/mastering limiter. It's very easy to use and sounds absolutely amazing. I use it for mastering as well as individual track limiting/clipping. It's incredibly flexible with multiple limiting algorithms, oversampling as well as adjustable attack and release settings. I've used a lot of different limiters over many years--this is the one that stayed and for good reason.

Visit: http://bit.ly/2ws1pJn

Multiband Compressors

FabFilter Pro-MB

This is my go to multiband compressor because it's the easiest to use. It's exquisitely transparent and musical sounding. I've used a lot of multiband compressors over the years—this one is King. With per-band sidechains, upwards and downwards compression/expansion it's the most flexible, easy to use multiband dynamic processor there is. As with all FabFilter plugins the visual interface is a cut above the rest.

Visit: http://bit.ly/2KK3Xp3

Multiband Distortion

Kombinat TRI

Too many multiband distortion processors are bloated with a confusing amount of features. I love the ease and simplicity of this one. I pretty much only use the Saturation, Clipping, Fuzz, and Tube Clip distortion algorithms with Saturation getting the heaviest use.

Visit: http://bit.ly/2FZvr6o

FXpansion Maul

This is actually the best and simultaneously most analog sounding multiband distortion out there. It's a little deeper than Kombinat TRI, but it's still the 2nd simplest multiband distortion out there. As far as I'm concerned FXpansion nailed the sound of this with their proprietary DCAM-modeled diode, tube and transistor based circuits along with clippers, overdrives and waveshapers. This thing is an absolute beast.

Visit: http://bit.ly/2jMjpoC

Modulation

Soundtoys PhaseMistress

I've tried more phasers than I can count and Phasemistress is the best. It can do every phasing sound you dream of. You really won't need to tweak it outside of frequency, depth and rate because of its more than 60+ phaser styles that you can select on the fly. If you're a tweaker then it also gives you access to much deeper controls as well.

Visit: http://bit.ly/2wBlRYn

Valhalla UberMod

This is categorically the best chorusing effect out there. It can do everything from chorusing to flanging as well as delays. It's an incredibly flexible and easy to use tool. Once upon a time I owned an Eventide H3000 and I look at this plugin as its twin brother.

Visit: http://bit.ly/2jMw1vZ

Xfer LFO Tool

Tremolo allows us to rhythmically shape the volume of a sound. Conventionally, tremolo is used for kick based sidechain compression. But LFO tool allows you to achieve much more exotic results. It allows for rhythmic control of volume, panning, and a variety of filters. Once you begin looking at tremolo as way to create rhythmic texture and movement within your projects it will completely change how you design and engineer your music.

Visit: http://bit.ly/2Iso2SE

Saturation

Soundtoys Radiator
I almost retired this plugin until I discovered its power on vocals. It can take a $100 mic recording and turn it into a $1000 dollar mic recording. I don't typically drive it very hard, but adding it to vocals and lightly turning up the hi-frequency gain instantly makes vocals cut through a mix like a hot knife through butter.

Visit: http://bit.ly/2G2g3pY

Virtual Console Collection 2.0
This plugin emulates the extremely musical and transparent saturation of analog consoles. Another secret you'd only find here: 50% of Nathan's super awesome sound is that he uses VCC feeding into FG-Grey on each of the 5 buses/groups described in *The Bus Compression Framework* (I use the same console emulation for all 5 groups but I don't use VCC on the master). So

Secret: All 5 buses: VCC > FG-Grey

Visit: http://bit.ly/2G0L5P5

Tape Simulation

Slate Digital Virtual Tape Machines

This is my favorite tape machine for saturating leads and anything that doesn't have sub (<100hz) energy in it. It's one of the best sounding tape emulations there is—I just wouldn't let it touch my basses because it pumps up the sub volume, for me, in an undesirable way. Nonetheless I use this as a warming and rounding tool for instruments that are too bright or sound to sterile. I literally just slap it on and sterility and brightness are cured.

Visit: http://bit.ly/2K82kAr

Transient Shaper

Oxford Transmod

This is the transient shaper to rule all transient shapers. It allows you to control the exact length and intensity of transient information within a signal. Something a lot of people don't think to do with these tools is to use them on leads, hi hats and other instruments where more/less attack is desired. This gives you a level of control over transient snap that no compressor can approach. Oxford Transmod is the only transient shaper

I know of that can effectively shape transients on instruments other than drums.

Visit: http://bit.ly/2wupq2c

Reverbs

Valhalla Room

This is my workhorse reverb. It's so flexible and easy to use that you can never go wrong with using it. In my opinion it's the best reverb for ambient styles as well as aggressive styles as the decay length can be set as long as you need. I'm a huge fan of this developer.

Visit: http://bit.ly/2KacFfp

Verbsuite Classics

Here's another Easter egg for you. In *The 3-Space Reverb Framework* I talk about how to use a Master reverb to glue your mix together. I also mentioned that your master reverb should be different from your other reverbs. This is my master reverb. It's perfect for anything with a shorter decay (<2sec). I don't feel it's strong for long-decay reverb like Valhalla Room. But the clarity, depth and space this reverb creates is 2nd to none which is why it's my Master reverb.

Visit: http://bit.ly/2wauPLU

Softube TSAR-1 Reverb

In my opinion this is the best reverb for drums. Its somewhat grainy texture makes it excellent for organic sources like Drums, Vocals and Keys. In *The 3-Space Reverb Framework* I talk about increasing depth by blending and contrasting different types of reverb units. As an example, whereas Valhalla Room is smooth and excels at blending, TSAR-1's grainy character is great for creating contrast and pushing instruments toward the front of your mix. I would avoid drenching an entire mix with TSAR-1 because it will devour your mixing real-estate fast. Just use it on 1, maybe two instruments or just drums and that should be it.

Visit: http://bit.ly/2I65U1i

Made in the USA
Coppell, TX
22 February 2023

13286754R00062